by
**Lindsay Anne O'Neal,
Tiffany Lynn Young**
+
Antonio Florencio Delgado Segundo

JUMP LITTLE CAKE, JUMP!

JUMP LITTLE CAKE, JUMP!

by
**Lindsay Anne O'Neal,
Tiffany Lynn Young**
+
Antonio Florencio Delgado Segundo

© 2012 The Happy Three, LLC
www.thehappy3llc.com
Austin,Texas

ISBN Book Goodness

Music by The Tiny Bots, www.thetinybots.com
© 2012 Tiny Bot Music [BMI]
& all that legal jargon

Printed in China
CPSIA Section 103 (a) Compliant
www.beaconstar.com/consumer
ID: M0120349. Tracking No.: M2212516-8732

We play nice, email us if you would like to use our materials.

www.jumplittlecake.com

ISBN-10: 0985838701
ISBN-13: 978-0-9858387-0-6

We'd like to dedicate this book to our parents, who always taught us to
Take Courage + Dream Big!

The O'Nilla family comes from a long line of cupcakes who live to celebrate the day—any day and every day. Fun is always on the top of the agenda.

Everything you assume about a cupcake is true. You have cupcakes for birthdays, baby showers, the last day of school, weddings, bar mitzvahs, bat mitzvahs, quinceañeras, sweet 16s, picnics, holidays and for straight A's. Cupcakes are there for you, and they bring the party with them.

Ask yourself, "Have I ever eaten a cupcake and been sad? Have I ever eaten a cupcake and cried?" Science has proven that the chances are 0.00062%, according to the University of Statistics, Chances and Greater Mathematics. And we all know that if science can prove it, it must be true.

So you might be wondering,

"HOW DOES A CUPCAKE CELEBRATE?"

WITH SPRINKLES, OF COURSE.

"Where is Preston?" Mama O'Nilla said.

"Yeah, where is he?" Frenchie questioned with anticipation. "It's time to celebrate and party! I mean, it's Thursday and it's his turn in the party calendar."

"YEAH, PARTY!" Bean exclaimed. Then the cupcakes broke into song and dance.

Then Papa O'Nilla stepped in and halted the song with a voice of reason, "Wait! We can't start without our special guest."

Without missing a beat, Bean began to wave his hands. "I think I see him there in the corner."

All the cupcakes turned to see Preston's back toward them. He was peering out of the container into the kitchen, and cleaning his glasses. As the newest member of the family, Preston completed the baker's dozen.

"Why don't we surprise him?" Bean proposed in a hushed tone. "Yeah! We could surprise him and it would be great!" he repeated, selling the idea to himself.

"We could surprise him. But isn't the party already on the calendar?" Frenchie questioned.

"We could surprise him because it's in the calendar!" Bean retorted.

"OK! EVERYONE GRAB YOUR SPRINKLES!" Mama O'Nilla exclaimed in excitement.

The crew of cupcakes quickly gathered their gear of happiness and snuck up behind Preston wearing blissful smiles.

"Surprise!" the cupcakes yelled as sprinkles filled the air like confetti at a concert.

"Ah ... thanks guys. Why don't you start the party without me?" Preston said timidly.

"Oh, but we are having the party in your honor 'cause it's Thursday!" Bean reminded him.

"Yeah, it's in the calendar!" Frenchie cited with her clipboard in hand.

"I know, but, it's just, well ... yeah, in a moment," Preston said and without hesitation, the remaining dozen went on to party without him.

As the party came to an end, Preston approached his parents with a solemn face.

"I have something to confess. I'm not like you. I'm not as fun. I like parties and I like sprinkles. I like you. But I can't pretend. I've got glasses, and I'm not made of vanilla, but pumpkin and spices. And I have to admit, sometimes I would rather just watch the fun instead of joining in," Preston said.

The crowd of cupcakes gasped so hard they nearly sucked the air out of their container.

"You know, son, you may be adopted, but you are still a cupcake. You are still an O'Nilla, but you need to know about the flavor that makes you distinctly you. And every cupcake knows they are here to share joy," his dad said.

"Does a cupcake ever have an excuse for not feeling like having a party? We each have our own talents. Frenchie does a great job keeping the calendar well organized, so our parties are never double booked. Bean's heart of spontaneity always helps bring the fun. You see son, we all have our place in the party," Papa O'Nilla explained.

That night, after everyone had gone to bed, Preston quietly snuck out of the container. Fear struck his heart as he had never left the container before. He had a hard time making out where he was in the darkness.

"Hey, watch your step. Some of us are trying to sleep," Salt snapped as she snuggled with Pepper.

"I'm so sorry," Preston whispered sheepishly.

For the next few minutes, Preston stood still like a deer in headlights. His frosting trembled as new sounds came from every direction.

Eventually, Preston stumbled past the napkin holder, and then traveled several more feet across the table.

For a cupcake, venturing out this far is a huge accomplishment. A foot to a cupcake would be the size of a city block to you and me.

Then, without notice, Preston almost lost his frosting. He made a shocking discovery: He had made it to the edge of the table. Few cupcakes had made it this far before, and even fewer knew what else was in the kitchen. For the most part, everyone kept to their own corner.

"SON, ARE YOU UP? AND DON'T YOU EVEN THINK ABOUT GETTING A CUPCAKE. IT'S PAST YOUR BEDTIME."

Preston quivered in fear behind the cookie jar. His mind was jumbled with images of what terrible things could happen next. Would he be seen? Who would find him? The kitchen was dark and cold, and he was beginning to want to turn around and just go home.

PSSSSSTHHHH....

The airtight seal of the cookie jar broke open.

"Oh, my little heart, a cupcake has lost his way! Hello, my dear. My name is Suga'. Why don't you come in from the cold and take a warm seat inside."

Before Preston could mutter a word, he was inside, sitting on a stool with a hot cup of cocoa with marshmallows bewildered and wanting to keep his thoughts to himself. But Suga' had a way with making people feel at ease. Her skin was golden and she was easy on the eyes and Preston became soft in her presence. He mentioned that he had felt out of place in the container with the others.

"The others? What do you mean, my dear? You look like a cupcake to me. Did Bundt send ya my way?"

"Bundt? Um, no. Bundt who?"

"Oh, don't ya worry about that. Why don't you hang your hat here tonight and I'll send you on your way in the morning?"

"But I don't have a hat."

"Don't worry about that ... In the morning, after you get some proper rest you can continue on your way. Get some rest now, little cake," Suga' said.

Preston woke up fresh. The warmth of the cookie jar helped him find a deep slumber. It was a new day and he was excited to embark on his adventure.

Suga' helped ease some of the greatest fears a cupcake can have. She leaned over and hugged Preston.

"NOW LISTEN UP, MY SWEETNESS. YOU KEEP YOUR EYES ON THE TOWER AT THE END OF THE COUNTER. YOU'LL KNOW WHEN YOU'VE GOTTEN TO THE RIGHT PLACE."

The kitchen may seem like a big place to someone as small as a cupcake. But Suga' gave it a small-town vibe. And for the first time, Preston felt like he had direction.

"Now mosey on down to the fridge, find Broc and tell him that Suga' sent you."

The journey to the end of the counter took longer than Preston expected.
Suga' had set his heart at ease, and because he felt calmer, Preston took in the sights along the way.

When Preston got to the edge of the counter, he hung his wrapper just over the edge. With the fridge in sight, Preston had no idea how he was going to get there. It was then that he overheard the canned goods whispering amongst themselves.

"Do you think the little cake is going to jump?"

"Yeah, I think he can make it!"

As they whispered amongst themselves, a chant broke out behind Preston.

JUMP-LITTLE-CAKE,-JUMP!
JUMP-LITTLE-CAKE,-JUMP!

JUMP-LITTLE-CAKE,-JUMP!
JUMP-LITTLE-CAKE,-JUMP!

JUMP-LITTLE-CAKE,-JUMP!
JUMP-LITTLE-CAKE,-JUMP!

JUMP-LITTLE-CAKE,-JUMP!

JUMP-LITTLE-CAKE,-JUMP!

Preston began to get excited. He even felt confident that he could make the jump.

"I can do it!" he told himself. He could jump. He could make it. Preston had never felt so courageous in his timid, short lifetime.

"Yeah, I can do it!" he cried aloud.

The chant had grown and enveloped him. He backed up a few steps and then ran his little body as fast as it would carry him. At the very last moment he launched himself as hard as he could toward the fridge.

The crowd cheered and Preston felt indestructible as he pushed himself away from the ledge.

A HUSH FELL OVER THE CROWD.

"IS HE OK?" the green beans whispered to the creamed corn.
Preston slid to the floor, not moving a single crumb.
Then Preston's frosting began to wiggle and he pulled himself up. The room filled with cheers.

"HOORAY! HE'S ALIVE! HOORAY! HE DID WHAT NO CUPCAKE HAS EVER DONE BEFORE! HE MADE IT!" they all cried.

Disappointed to see his glasses broken, he took a bit of frosting to set his glasses straight.
Preston was embarrassed, yet the cheers from the crowd gave him courage.

"PASSWORD!" Milk said in a booming voice.

THEN THE DOOR SLAMMED SHUT.

"Password?" thought Preston. "What password?" Preston was having a hard time thinking as he was still putting himself back together.

KNOCK KNOCK KNOCK

"Do you have the password?" Milk said impatiently.

"Um ... well ... uh ... yeah ... I don't know. How about ...
3/4 cup butter, softened
2 ½ cup sugar
3 eggs
1 can 15 ounce solid pumpkin
1/2 tablespoon vanilla
2 1/3 cup cake flour"

Preston had always done well in school, and he thought a recipe might appease Milk, because everyone is always looking for a good pumpkin spice cake recipe.

"What? We're not making a cake here," Milk said.

Preston then thought back to his family and resorted to what he knew best, "Um ... Surprise!!!!!"

Milk pondered what he was dealing with. "Listen, you're a sweet cupcake, but we have rules around here, and no one gets in without the password. So, either tell me the password or I'm going to have to send you back to where you came from. Where did you come from?"

The cupcake began to quiver with nervousness.

"Well, I'm from the cupcake container, but I just came from Suga's place a moment ago and she told me to talk to Broc, because I left my family because I don't fit in and they threw me a surprise party because it was Thursday and I didn't want to party and they knew it so I told them I was different and I'm trying to find my true flavor," Preston explained quickly in a single breath.

"Hold on there, little cake," Milk interrupted. "If Suga' sent you, why didn't you say so? Anyone that's a friend of Suga's is a friend of mine, and boy do I have a soft spot for sweets! But next time you need to have the password, little one. It's 'Bundt,' of course, but don't be telling anyone," he said as he held the door open for Preston.

"BUNDT!" Preston exclaimed.
"SUGA' MENTIONED BUNDT, TOO! WHO IS THAT?"

"I am sure you'll find out soon enough, little cake, but for now, I need to show you the way to Broc like Suga' requested. I know my way around the fridge like the back of my nutrition label," he said. "Come this way."

Preston was overwhelmed as he saw things he had never seen before—little berries, round and blue, strawberries, pears and apples, too.

Milk showed Preston off to everyone along the way, pointing out who was who in the fruit basket. Finally, they arrived at the Crisper. Turnip was watching the door.

"WHERE IS BROC?" Milk asked.

"OH, HE'S IN THE BACK. GO ON THROUGH," Turnip replied.

Suddenly Preston heard a steady beat and as they came upon the Beet-niks, he could hear a flow of words being flung from one to the other.

"THE MEANING OF LIFE IS BOOKS
AND FINDING A LITTLE NOOK
TO SIP A CUP OF JOE - YOU KNOW
DELIBERATIN', PUNCTUATIN'
AND TAKING THE TIME TO EVALUATE—"

They noticed mid-thought that they were not alone.

"Oh, hey 2 percent, who's this you have with you?" Vitamin A, the carrot, asked.

"This is Preston. Suga' sent him—says he's lost or something. Ran away from home. Looking for flavor. Thought you might be able to help."

"Well, sure. We all ran away, too. We'll show him the ropes," Broc said.

With that, Milk said he had a carb craving and needed to get away from Preston before he did anything he'd regret.

"Oh, come on, Milk. We all know you have a sweet tooth, but you'd never hurt a cute little cupcake," said the tall asparagus, who they all knew as Gus.

Preston was excited to meet the group. They all welcomed him immediately. He had never met a group as hip as they were before. They stayed up late at night talking about what life outside the fridge must be like, how fruits are different from veggies, and why kiwis are fuzzy.

Time passed quickly, as he never knew if it was day or night inside the Crisper.

Although Preston came to see them as brothers, he still knew he couldn't stay forever. He cared about them, but he knew this was not his home, so he approached the group one night.

"I think it's time for me to go," Preston said.

"We're all going somewhere," Gus said.

"Yeah, one day I might be going to make carrot juice," Vitamin A said.

"And one day I'll be covered in cheese," Broc said.

"Satisfying taste buds, because we aim to please," Gus carried on.

And the Beet-niks snapped to the beat, egging one another on for each new rhyme.

Without skipping a beat, Preston jumped in.

"I hope you'll understand. I need to find my place.
I've loved my time with you, but my journey must continue.
I'm looking for something grand. A purpose and knowledge of who I am.
I know I have a meaning in life but thus far I'm still looking for something more."

They snapped into applause. Preston had grown so much in the short time they had known him. It was the first time he had jumped into the beat. They would miss him, but Broc knew it was the right thing to do.

"Oh, Little Cake, you've come a long way. You might be right. It may be time for you to go. If you're searching for flavor I know the place. It's a bit of a journey, but you'll grow along the way. You'll find a path to the freezer behind the thermostat. Once in the freezer, you'll find a secret passage behind the ice machine. Then it's straight up from there, where you'll find our all-knowing friend Bundt. He'll take it from there."

When Preston arrived atop the fridge, he saw a big, round piece of cake. He'd never seen a cake of such grandeur.

"He must be Bundt!" Preston thought. "Who else would be on top of the fridge?"

It was clear he had been around a while, with crumbs and pieces scattered about. He was sound asleep and snoring, without a care.

Preston waited and waited and waited for him to come to, but finally he realized he must be courageous. He had to wake up Bundt.

He stood there for a moment, pulling together all the courage he had in his thick frosting coat. When he finally went to open his lips, the tiniest whisper fell, "Bundt … are you awake?"

"BUNDT ARE YOU AWAKE?"

"That's not courage," Preston reprimanded himself and then straightened his swirl. "I need to be bold. I need to be flavorful. I need to be a cupcake."

That's when he said it. It just came out fast: "Bundt—I'm a cupcake and Preston is your friend."

"I NEED TO BE BOLD.
I NEED TO BE FLAVORFUL.
I NEED TO BE A CUPCAKE."

Bundt woke up with a start. "What did you say little one?"

"Um. I'm a cupcake, and I'm gonna be your friend."

"Straightforward … I like that. It seems like you've come a long way. I have been watching your adventures since you left the container. Preston, let me tell you—your dad and I go back as far as the mixer. You have a loving family—look at them wave."

Preston looked at the table he had come from and felt fulfilled. In that moment, he understood. He realized what made a complete recipe. Life is all about adding the right ingredients. Flour doesn't make bread without butter, salt and yeast.

'This is my family,' he told himself. 'I am an O'Nilla. I may not be the life of the party, but I know what it's like to feel left out.'

"From now on, I know my place in this world of cupcakes, and that is to include everyone in the kitchen," Preston said aloud.

"You've completed your journey. You are now very wise, my friend. I think you should join your family. How about a surprise?" Bundt asked.

Preston looked around. "How will I get down there?" he asked.

"There are ways," Bundt said with a glint in his eyes.

Preston knew he had to be creative. Behind Bundt, he saw a stack of napkins. Preston raced over, grabbed two tips of the first napkin he saw, and with a smile on his face, he said, "Goodbye! It's my time to fly."

"SURPRISE!" Preston shouted as his wrapper landed softly.

"SURPRISE!" his family shouted back.

Papa O'Nilla stepped forward. "We've been waiting for you, son."

"I'm an O'Nilla, Dad. I may be different, but I'm a cupcake, too," Preston shouted.

"I know, son. You were all along."

At that, sprinkles flew, and confetti filled the air. It was the best party the O'Nillas had ever had.

WELL, SINCE THE LAST PARTY, ANYWAY.

THE END!

THANK YOU!!!
FRIENDS OF PRESTON:

Alice Gahbauer

Amy Stabeno

Tony and Rose Delgado

Ashley

Barry and Norma O'Neal

Belinda Morales Walker

Benjamin F. Stewart III

Bren and Robert Young

Brenda Trafton

Colette White

Caitlin DeWeezy

Carmela Morales

Cheese

CoCo Young

cpchristine

Dana Anderson

Debbie Dudensing

Delilah Bellar

Donelle Harder

Eric and Lisa Pulsifer

Gib Brown

Heather Lambert

Heather Norman

Iris Galvan

J

Jacolin McAfoos

James and Cassie Bowen

Jane Cornelius

Jason Delgado

Jay O'Neal

Jennifer Huddleston

Jenny K.

Jeremiah Spoon

Jill Leonhart

John Dickerson

Joni

Jose and Rosa Escalante

Joshua Hernandez

Julie Allcorn

Karen J Lee

Kaysi O.

Kela Short

Kendall "Rocky" Cusick

Kendall Neck

Kinley Healey

Kristina Ambrosius

LaDonna Coursey &
    Jaylie Coursey

Lauren Itz

Lauren Lefrance

Leah Prescott

Leslie Avila

Linda and Carl Alford

Linda Thaxton

THANK YOU!!!
FRIENDS OF PRESTON:

Lindsey McCrary

Lynette Mixon

Mark R. Collins

Macy D. Hurwitz

Maggie Ruthless

Maria Brooks

Mark Taylor

Mary Walsh

Melissa

Melissa Riley

Monte Monreal

Myra Kay Jones

Nathan Cole DeWitt

Nathan, Meg, Addie and
Elliott O'Neal

Noah, Megan and Anisa
Morales

Pam and Dane Welch

Paula Avirett

Paula and Randy O'Neal

Phil Ju

Rick Hernandez

Rob Heidrick

Robert Adams

Robert Young

Rol Ortega

Rosanna Williams

Russell Bridges

Sarah Carlan

Shane Stapleton

Shannon Will

Simon Welch

Stephen & David

Steve & Barbara Russell

Sunny Kim

Tatiana

Teresa Gollihugh

Teri Noyes

Tina Sauer

Vena Leatherwood

Yvonne Lim Wilson

Zack Teibloom

Thank you to all of those listed here, who contributed to our Kickstarter campaign at the "Friends of Preston" level and above.

We couldn't have done this without you!

PRESTON PUMPKIN SPICE CUPCAKE RECIPE

Cupcake

3/4 cup butter, softened
2 ½ cup sugar
3 eggs
1 can 15 ounce solid pumpkin
1/2 tablespoon vanilla
2 1/3 cup cake flour
¼ cup ground almonds
1 teaspoon baking powder
½ teaspoon baking soda
1 teaspoon cinnamon
¾ teaspoon salt
½ teaspoon cardamom
¼ teaspoon nutmeg
¼ cup milk
¼ cup raisins

Frosting

3 cups confectioners sugar
1 cup butter, softened
1 teaspoon vanilla extract
1 teaspoon cardamom
1 tablespoon of milk

Directions

Preheat oven to 350 degrees.

Using a mixer, cream butter and sugar together in a large bowl. Beat in eggs, one at a time. Mix in pumpkin and vanilla. In a separate mixing bowl, combine flour, almonds, baking powder, baking soda and spices. Slowly add in flour mixture to pumpkin mixture until well combined. Add milk and combine well. Fold in raisins with a spatula. Pour batter into lined cupcake pans about ¾ full. Bake for 20 to 25 minutes, or until an inserted toothpick comes out clean.

Frosting

In a mixer, cream butter. Add confectioners sugar, vanilla and cardamom to butter until well-blended and creamy. Add a tablespoon of milk and beat if consistency of frosting is too thick. If needed, add another tablespoon.
When cupcakes are completely cool throughout, frost with a spatula or by piping the frosting onto the cupcake.

Optional

Garnish with sliced almonds and sprinkle with cinnamon.

THE HAPPY THREE

Tiffany Lynn Young

Tiffany loves cupcakes, crafting and writing. Tiffany has a degree in journalism, was an editor and writer at a community newspaper for several years and has also worked as a graphic designer. She obsessively devours books and is learning to play the ukulele. Tiffany is available for writing, editing, photography and design projects. Follow her latest adventures at tiffanylynnyoung.com.

Antonio Florencio Delgado

Antonio loves cupcakes, music and browsing craigslist for the low-priced, high-quality music and photography gear. He has taught journalism, has an engineering degree and makes pedals for musicians when he's not playing in a band, running or taking photos for the food blog ohspooning.com. He is available for building pedals and teaching songwriting. Discover his talents at ohantoniodelgado.com.

Lindsay Anne O'Neal

Lindsay loves cupcakes, planning creative, themed parties and collaboration. Lindsay, who came up with the idea for "Jump Little Cake, Jump," has a degree in art and did all the illustrations for the book. When she's not coming up with book ideas, she's crafting and painting. She is available for other illustration and art projects as well.
See her latest art projects at lindsayoneal.com.

THE MAKING OF PRESTON

WHAT NERDY CUPCAKES THINK ABOUT

VOICE OF THE NARRATOR

MAKING OF THE KICKSTARTER VIDEO

PRESTON STICKERS

THE VOICES OF SUGA' AND PRESTON

VOICE OF TURNIP

VOICE OF GREEN BEANS

HOPPY EASTER COLORING PAGE

CUPCAKES FOR KICKSTARTER SUPPORTERS

LAYOUT/DESIGNING THE BOOK

CREDITS

A special thanks goes out to those who helped us edit the book and did character audio voices.

Editing	Rob Heidrick
Music	The Tiny Bots
Engineering, mixed & mastered	Antonio Florencio Delgado Segundo
Assistant engineer, design & layout	Tiffany Lynn Young
Illustrations	Lindsay Anne O'Neal

CHARACTER VOICES

Narration	Kelly M. Whitenack
Preston	Antonio Florencio Delgado Segundo
Frenchie	Tiffany Lynn Young
Bean	Gene Davis
Papa O'Nilla	Benjamin F. Stewart III
Mama O'Nilla	Melissa Mixon
Broc	Mark R. Collins
Carrot	Ranjana Thomas
Gus	Nick Warrenchuk
Turnip	Heath Robinson
Human mom	Kelsey Robinson
Salt	Lisa Pulsifer
Suga	Heather Lee Calvillo
Milk	Rich Vasquez
Bundt	Eric Pulsifer
Green beans	Lindsay Anne O'Neal
Can #1	Skipper McWithey
Can #2	Preston McWithey
"The Sprinkles Song"	Tiffany Lynn Young, Melissa Mixon and Gene Davis
"It's a Great Big Kitchen"	Heather Lee Calvillo and Antonio Florencio Delgado Segundo
"Shake it Like a Cupcake"	Tiffany Lynn Young and Antonio Florencio Delgado Segundo

AUDIO TRACK

SOUND EFFECTS CREDITS

"Household Refrigerator"
R Humphries

"Salt"
Melack

"Acoustic Bass Loop"
Harri

"Dripping Faucet"
Sazman

"Opening Jar"
Fonogeno

"Lightbulb Wink"
FreqMan

"Gasp"
FreqMan

"Refrigerator Hum"
DigiFishMusic

"Enthusiastic Audience"
LoneMonk

"Running"
SageTyrtle

"Air Conditioner"
Uncle Sigmond

"FootSteps"
Corsica S

"Snoring"
Smidoid

"Fingersnap"
SandyRB

"Dragging Feet"
Wentzelj

"Snapping His Fingers"
Mario1298